ACTIVATING THE FORCES OF VENGEANCE

God, put an end to evil; avenging God, show your colors! Judge of the earth, take your stand; throw the book at the arrogant.

Psalm 94:1-2 *MSG*

by
Franklin N. Abazie

Activating the Forces of Vengeance
COPYRIGHT 2016 BY Franklin N Abazie
ISBN: 978-1-94513315-2

All right reserved. This book or any portion thereof may not be reproduced or used in any manner whatsoever without the express written permission of the publisher, except for the use of brief quotations in a book review. All Bible quotes are from King James Version and others as noted.

Published by: F N ABAZIE PUBLISHING HOUSE—aka, Empowerment Bookstore

That I may publish with the voice of thanksgiving and tell of all thy wondrous works.
Psalm 26:7

To order additional copies, wholesales or booking call:
the Church office (973-372-7518)
or Empowerment Bookstore Hotline (973-393-8518)

Worship address:
343 Sanford Avenue, Newark, New Jersey 07106
Administrative Head Office address:
33 Schley Street Newark New Jersey 07112
Email: pastorfranknto@yahoo.com
Website www.fnabaziehealingministries.org
Publishing House: www.fnabaziepublishinghouse.org

This book is a production of F N Abazie Publishing House. A publication Arms of Miracle of God Ministries 2016.
First Edition

CONTENTS

THE MANDATE OF THE COMMISSION......................iv
ARMS OF THE COMMISSION..........................……....v
INTRODUCTION...vi
CHAPTER 1
The Forces of Vengeance…………......................…...1
CHAPTER 2
Overcoming the Tribulations of Life.......................18
CHAPTER 3
Conquering the Forces of Wickedness...................30
CHAPTER 4
Prayer of Salvation..55
CHAPTER 5
About the Author...66

THE MANDATE OF THE COMMISSION

"The moment is due to impact your world through the revival of the healing & miracle ministry of Jesus Christ of Nazareth.

"I am sending you to restore health unto thee and I will heal thee of thy wounds, said the Lord of Host."

ARMS OF THE COMMISSION

1) F N Abazie Ministries—Miracle of God Ministries (Miracle Chapel Intl)

2) F N Abazie TV Ministries: Global Television Ministry Outreach

3) F N Abazie Radio Ministries: Radio Broadcasting Outreach

4) F N Abazie Publishing House: Book Publication

5) F N Abazie Bible School: also called Word of Healing Bible School (W.O.H.B.S.)

6) F N Abazie Evangelistic Ass: Miracle of God Ministries: Global Crusade

7) Empowerment Bookstore: Book distribution

8) F N Abazie Helping Hands: Meeting the Help of the Needy Worldwide

9) F N Abazie Disaster Recovery Mission: Global Disaster Recovery

10) F N Abazie Prison Ministry: Prison Ministry For All Convicts "Second Chance"

Some of our ministry arms are awaiting the appointed time to commence.

INTRODUCTION

It is believed that if you are a believer, you must be polite, soft- spoken, seek for peace among men at all times and always seeking for the good of others. As believer we are admonished from the scriptures to live a righteous lifestyle, to imitate the life of CHRIST. There are troublemakers in our families and in our communities, who will never allow peace to reign nor allow us to occupy our lawful and rightful position in any aspect of life. "If you are a Christian, it does not mean you are a weak person." Silence also over any offense or trial in life does not mean weakness. As an African, I have witnessed various forms of torture, abuse and molestation growing up as a young man. The HOLY SPIRIT compelled and convicted me to write this book, ACTIVATING THE FORCES OF VENGEANCE, out of my own personal life challenges and experiences.

And from the days of John the Baptist until now the kingdom of heaven suffers violence, and the violent take it by force.
Matthew 11:12

We live in a spiritually violent era, where wickedness has been accepted as the norm of the day. The devil have crept into our hearts and is causing tribulation to God's own special people. If we do not rise up to fight back with the sword of the spirit, which is the word of God—(see Ephesians 6:17)—the enemy will win the spiritual battles over our lives and destinies. It is time for us all to pray differently. We must storm offensive bombarding vengeance prayers into the throne room of Jehovah-God.

Harass these hecklers, God, punch these bullies in the nose. Grab a weapon, anything at hand; stand up for me!
Psalm 35:1-3 MSG

Although we live in a civilized society, so many people have died not only because of their faith, but because they were quiet and did nothing about the prevailing attack against them from human agents, sent by the devil. It is time to put God's army at work.

Unless the Lord had given me help, I would soon have dwelt in the silence of death.
Psalm 94:17

God, put an end to evil; avenging God, show your colors! Judge of the earth, take your stand; throw the book at the arrogant. God, the wicked get away with murder—how long will you let this go on?

They brag and boast and crow about their crimes! They walk all over your people, God, exploit and abuse your precious people. They take out anyone who gets in their way; if they can't use them, they kill them. They think, "God isn't looking, Jacob's God is out to lunch."
Psalm 94:1-7 MSG

In Nigeria for example, there are ritual killers almost everywhere in the country, kidnappers. There are evil men and women who will happily go an extra mile to kill and destroy any believer who is prospering and doing well in life. In the Eastern part of Nigeria, for example, real estate land disputes have sent so many precious people into their early graves.

We must all **ACTIVATE THE FORCES OF VENGEANCE** against any prevailing assault from the mouth of the enemy. Unless vengeance shows up, evil men and women will never cease from their evil activities nor repent of their evil doings. Most evil men and women quickly run to a fetish priest or voodoo doctor to acquire diabolic black power that they will use to subdue and overcome the soft-spoken peacemaker called a believer. These men and women are evil because there is no instant judgment from God—they will never cease nor stop from their demonic activities.

Because sentence against an evil work is not executed speedily, therefore the heart of the sons of men is fully set in them to do evil.
Ecclesiastes 8:11

The vengeance God must show up to avenge for us against all the wiles and schemes of the adversary-the Devil. **EVIL MEN WILL NEVER REPENT.**

Oh let the wickedness of the wicked come to an end; but establish the just: for the righteous God trieth the hearts and reins.
Psalm 7:9

The wickedness of the wicked will prevail unless we are determined to stir up the spirit of vengeance.

And shall not God avenge his own elect, which cry day and night unto him, though he bear long with them? I tell you that he will avenge them speedily.
Luke 18:7-8

Because sentence against an evil work is not executed speedily, therefore the heart of the sons of men is fully set in them to do evil.
Ecclesiastes 8:11

I concluded a long time ago that if we do not activate the forces of vengeance, evil will continue to prevail. **The Bible says in Genesis 8:22: *"... for the imagination of man's heart is evil from his youth."*** And in Eccesiastes 8:13: *"But it shall not be well with the wicked, neither shall he prolong his days, which are as a shad-*

ow; because he feareth not before God." I have learned that when the vengeance God shows up, all evil plots are subdued and paralyzed. It is my desire to see the vengeance of God show up even as you progress reading this book.

VENGEANCE BELONGS TO GOD

Dearly beloved, avenge not yourselves, but rather give place unto wrath: for it is written, Vengeance is mine; I will repay, saith the Lord.
Romans 12:19

A lot of us have misinterpreted and misrepresented the above and below scriptures. "Vengeance belongs to GOD" but we have a great role to play. In my own interpretation, When the bible says "vengeance belongs unto GOD" it is only a proposition. We as a believer, with the accreditation to enforce the LAWS of the SPIRIT must activate that proposition by praying offensively.

But I say unto you, That ye resist not evil: but whosoever shall smite thee on thy right cheek, turn to him the other also. And if any man will sue thee at the law, and take away thy coat, let him have thy cloak also. And whosoever shall compel thee to go a mile, go with him twain.
Mathew 5:39-41

We as believers must rise up to all prevailing

challenges in life. "That vengeance belongs to God" does not mean we must be quiet and silent. We live in a material world where you only get what you are ready to fight for. We must face the reality of life and oppose those who oppose us like David said in Psalm 35:1, and contend with those who contend with us.

ACTIVATING THE FORCES OF VENGEANCE IS RIGHTEOUS

Seeing it is a righteous thing with God to recompense tribulation to them that trouble you.
2 Thessalonians 1:6

Let no one fool you. Unless you fight back spiritually, you are heading for defeat. We must all pray offensive prayers and chase the enemy into the pit. In my opinion, activating the forces of evil is the right thing to do—especially if you have ever been troubled by any wicked man or woman, witches or wizards.

ACTIVATING THE FORCES OF VENGENACE GRANTS PROTECTION

From henceforth let no man trouble me: for I bear in my body the marks of the Lord Jesus.
Galatians 6:17

Unless we activate the forces of vengeance and

pray offensive prayers, we will remain a prey in the mouth of the enemy. The reason for all the trouble and trauma is because there is no covering over our lives. Otherwise, if God truly be for you, who can be against you?

> *What shall we then say to these things?*
> *If God be for us, who can be against us?*
> **Romans 8:31**

Every time you pray offensive violent prayers, you keep the enemy far from your life. Unless otherwise stated, until you activate the forces of vengeance through offensive violent prayers, you will never break through in life. So many great lives and destines have been caged by the bond woman.

I therefore pray against all evil curses, incantations, enchantments, sorceries, negative prophecies, the sun of the bondwoman, marabouts, occultists, satanic watchmen, activated or programmed into the sun, the moon, the stars, Pleiades, Orion, Mazzaroth, Arcturus by the blood of Jesus Christ of Nazareth. I see you **ACTIVATING THE FORCES OF VENGENACE** as you read this book. Rejoice and be glad for the LORD will do GREAT things.

HAPPY READING!

*But do thou for me, O God the Lord,
for thy name's sake: because thy mercy is good,
deliver thou me.
For I am poor and needy,
and my heart is wounded within me.
I am gone like the shadow when it declineth:
I am tossed up and down as the locust.
My knees are weak through fasting;
and my flesh faileth of fatness.
I became also a reproach unto them:
when they looked upon me they shaked their heads.
Help me, O Lord my God:
O save me according to thy mercy:
That they may know that this is thy hand;
that thou, Lord, hast done it.
Let them curse, but bless thou:
when they arise, let them be ashamed;
but let thy servant rejoice.
Let mine adversaries be clothed with shame,
and let them cover themselves
with their own confusion, as with a mantle.
I will greatly praise the Lord with my mouth;
yea, I will praise him among the multitude.
For he shall stand at the right hand of the poor,
to save him from those that condemn his soul.*
Psalm 109:21-31

HIGHLIGHTS

HOW TO ACTIVATE
THE FORCES OF VENGEANCE

RIGHTEOUSNESS

*And he shall judge the world in righteousness,
he shall minister judgment to the people in uprightness.*
Psalm 9:8

*Then justice will dwell in the wilderness,
and righteousness remain in the fruitful field.
The work of righteousness will be peace;
and the effect of righteousness,
quietness and assurance forever.*
Isaiah 32:16-17

I cannot overemphasize the supernatural outcome of living a lifestyle of RIGHTEOUSNESS—doing what is right at all times, not sometimes, but always doing the right thing at any place, at any time. It takes a sincere and a pure conscience to practice RIGHTEOUSNESS. David said, "I have done judgment and justice: leave me not to mine oppressors."

As long as you are innocent—meaning your hands are cleansed from any evil accusation, court cases or demonic attacks—the evil one will not prevail over your circumstance. The prerequisite for the **ACTIVATION OF THE FORCES OF VENGEANCE** is living a righteous life.

> *And who is he that will harm you,*
> *if ye be followers of that which is good?*
> *1 Peter 3:13*

> *Whoso keepeth the commandment shall*
> *feel no evil thing: and a wise man's heart discerneth*
> *both time and judgment.*
> **Ecclesiastes 8:5**

FAITH IS OUR VICTORY CERTIFICATION

> *For whatsoever is born of God overcometh*
> *the world: and this is the victory that overcometh*
> *the world, even our faith.*
> **1 John 5:4**

We do not stand a chance to prevail against the enemy in life unless FAITH takes its RIGHTFUL perspective in our lives. FAITH is our VICTORY CERTIFICATION against all the brutal attacks of the devil. It is the mystery of faith that will subdue and overcome the wicked one (the devil). It is established that without faith we cannot please God. Hebrews 11:6 attested to this truth. There is no way we can activate the forces of vengeance without genuine FAITH and TRUST in God. Most prevailing attacks from the enemy against our lives began when we allowed the spirit of fear to enter into our heart. Unless we develop faith, we cannot activate the forces of vengeance.

Above all, taking the shield of faith, wherewith ye shall be able to quench all the fiery darts of the wicked.
Ephesians 6:16

FAITH is a shield (covering) that protects us from the assaults of the enemy. Therefore, you must develop faith that will crush all prevailing evil forces. The reason for all the devastation and destruction Job suffered was a result of fear.

For the thing which I greatly feared is come upon me, and that which I was afraid of is come unto me.
Job 3:25

PRAYER

But ye beloved, building up your selves on your most holy faith, praying in the Holy Ghost.
Jude 1:20

There is a mystery associated with Praying sincerely in the SPIRIT with all SUPPLICATION. What we do in prayers is to bombard the kingdom of hell, and to crush all prevailing plots and assaults from the camp of the enemy. Unless we open our mouth and say something violently in prayers, we will be defeated by the devil.

> *I am the Lord thy God, which brought thee out of the land of Egypt: open thy mouth wide, and I will fill it.*
> **Psalm 81:10**

God gave us a mouth to speak out against all violent attacks of the enemy.

> *For I will give you a mouth and wisdom, which all your adversaries shall not be able to gainsay nor resist.*
> **Luke 21:15**

PRAYER POINT TO ACTIVATE THE FORCES OF VENGENACE

1) O lord GOD, respond to me by your power.

2) Oppose those that oppose my life & destiny in Jesus name.

3) Holy Ghost fire, destroy all my contenders and opposers in the mighty name of Jesus.

4) Blood of Jesus, demolish any wall of hindrance and delay upon my life in the mighty name of Jesus.

5) Power of god, it is time to defend me in the name of Jesus.

6) Vengeance God, humiliate my enemies in the mighty name of Jesus.

7) Fire of god, roast my contenders in the mighty name of Jesus.

8) Fire of god, burn every wheat and chaff intimidating my success in the mighty name of Jesus.

9) Hand of God, revive my destiny in the mighty name of Jesus.

10) Omnipotent god, prove your hand upon my life by crushing my enemies in the mighty name of Jesus.

11) Unchangeable God, show your mighty hand of deliverance upon my life in the name of Jesus.

12) Mighty God of Jacob, divide the tongue of my enemies in the mighty name of Jesus.

13) Power of God, hijack all manipulating forces remoting my life in the name of Jesus.

14) Merciful God, have mercy upon my life in the name of Jesus.

15) Blood of Jesus, drown and silence all my mockers in the mighty name of Jesus.

16) Refiner's fire, baptize me with your supernatural power in the name of Jesus.

17) Ancient of days, catapult me into greatness in the name of Jesus.

18) Vengeance god, arise and scatter all my enemies in the name of Jesus.

19) Arise, oh God, let my enemies be scattered.

20) Holy Spirit, help me to live righteously before all men in the name of Jesus.

21) Holy Spirit, control my life. I yield myself to thee in the name of Jesus.

22) Precious Holy Spirit, garment my life.

23) Oh lord, let me overtake all those ahead of me in this race of life.

24) Lord God, baptize me with your spirit of humility.

VENGEANCE VERDICT

The good news about vengeance prayers is that it does not take too long. But it takes the quick VENGEANCE GOD, A FEW SECONDS to respond on our behalf. I guarantee you, before you finish reading this material there shall be desired good news for you IN THE NAME OF JESUS.

O Lord God, to whom vengeance belongeth;
O God, to whom vengeance belongeth, shew thyself.
Lift up thyself, thou judge of the earth:
render a reward to the proud.
Lord, how long shall the wicked,
how long shall the wicked triumph?
PSALM 94:1-3

It takes the understanding of the mysteries of vengeance to truly provoke and activate the forces of vengeance in our lives. God is the judge of the whole earth the Bible declares. (See Genesis 18:25.) Remember, God is not a partial God. (See Romans 2:11, Acts 10:34.) Whatever He did for one, He will do for all. **The Bible says** *"there is no difference between the Jews and the Greek, for the same Lord over all is rich unto all that call upon him."* (Romans 10:12)

After you have prayed, I admonish you to create time to worship, to reverence and to offer thanksgiving unto GOD.

CHAPTER 1
THE FORCES OF VENGEANCE

God is jealous, and the Lord revengeth;
the Lord revengeth, and is furious;
the Lord will take vengeance on his adversaries,
and he reserveth wrath for his enemies.
Nahum 1:2

WHAT IS VENGEANCE?

The American college heritage dictionary defines VENGEANCE as: *Infliction of punishment in return for a wrong retribution.* As long as no one has offended you, as long as men have done you well, as long as others have gone out of their way to help and comfort you in peace, you are not qualified to provoke the forces of vengeance. But if you have been molested, tortured and humiliated by an individual or gods (deity), you are the PERFECT candidate to activate the forces of vengeance.

HAVE YOU EVER BEEN HURT, OFFENDED OR MALTREATED?

The Forces of Vengeance, in my own understanding, are the platform for our total liberty. The perpetrator will never retreat unless counteroffensive proclamations are made to GOD in PRAYERS.

Vengeance prayers mean enforcing the laws of the spirit, the ability to skillfully bargain before ELOHIM and to prove our case before the RIGHTEOUS JUDGE. We must therefore give genuine reasons in PRAYERS why GOD should intervene. We must produce our reasons why GOD should afflict punishment on any individual or deity, in return for any wrong retribution against us.

The ALMIGHTY GOD reacts by inflicting vengeance punishment on any perpetrator who molested and tortured us in life. The wrath of vengeance is provoked especially when we communicate sincerely unto GOD, sincerely from the heart with tears about the prevailing oppression.

....for he that toucheth you toucheth the apple of his eye.
Zechariah 2:8

*When they went from one nation to another,
from one kingdom to another people;
He suffered no man to do them wrong:
yea, he reproved kings for their sakes;
Saying, Touch not mine anointed,
and do my prophets no harm.*
Psalm 105:13-15

One may ask, does GOD kill?

GOD KILLS AND MAKES ALIVE

Chapter 1 — The Forces of Vengeance

The Lord killeth, and maketh alive:
he bringeth down to the grave, and bringeth up.
1 Samuel 2:6

The greatest attribute of GOD is that **"He is OMNIPOTENT."** GOD has ability to create, destroy or make alive.

I form the light, and create darkness: I make peace, and create evil: I the Lord do all these things.
Isaiah 45:7

Think of this scripture....

And I say unto thee, Let my son go, that he may serve me: and if thou refuse to let him go, behold, I will slay thy son, even thy firstborn.
Exodus 4:23

Although most of us claim to be children of the MOST HIGH GOD, God responds to us all, based on our RIGHTEOUSNESS. The reason God appeared to ABIMELECH in a dream was because of Abraham's righteousness. *But God came to Abimelech in a dream by night, and said to him, Behold, thou art but a dead man, for the woman which thou hast taken; for she is a man's wife.* (Genesis 20:3) *And he believed in the Lord; and he counted it to him for righteousness.* (Genesis 15:6)

You will never stand a chance to activate nor provoke the vengeance God into action until you develop a lifestyle of RIGHTEOUSNESS.

WHY DO WE USE THE FORCES OF VENGEANCE?

Vengeance is our redemptive honor. It is our redemptive right to execute vengeance upon the wicked.

> *To execute vengeance upon the heathen,*
> *and punishments upon the people.*
> **Psalm 149:7**

> *This honour have all his saints. Praise ye the Lord.*
> **Psalm 149:9**

The Bible says that vengeance of God is a righteous thing with GOD. (See 2 Thessalonians 1:6.)

> *Oh let the wickedness of the wicked come to an end;*
> *but establish the just: for the righteous*
> *God trieth the hearts and reins.*
> **PSALM 7:9**

There are a few weapons, when in the right perspective, accelerates the wrath of God to release the forces of vengeance with SPEED. For example: Whenever we PRAISE GOD sincerely out of a pure heart with a clear conscience, GOD is bound to respond and intervene on our behalf with SPEED.

If we desire the wrath of GOD to be activated

on any prevailing circumstances, these few attributes must be established in our lives. Examples are the help of PRAISE, BOLDNESS, PURITY, FAITH, HOPE, ENDURANCE, JOY, PATIENCE, etc. in our lives.

If the fruit of the SPIRIT is not established in our lives, we cannot activate the forces of vengeance into action on any given circumstance. You cannot do wrong and at the same time want GOD to fight for you. There is no way you will steal and cheat and expect the backing of the most high God to afflict vengeance on your persecutors. We must be spiritual and righteous at the same time. There is no way GOD will defend a thief, for example. If you steal and are caught, you must be persecuted by the due process of the law.

Let's briefly examine these few weapons of vengeance.

WHAT ARE THE WEAPONS OF VENGEANCE?

PRAISE

> *For God is the King of all the earth:*
> *sing ye praises with understanding.*
> **Psalms 47:7**

Praise is a mystery of vengeance if provoked appropriately. Let's briefly examine the different dimensions of PRAISE that will ACTIVATE VENGEANCE:

1) PRAISE FOR DELIVERANCE: It is a vengeance mystery to activate praise, especially in time of tribulation and difficulty. Although Paul and Silas prayed, not until they praised did God come down. When they began to sing praises, the vengeance of God responded for their deliverance. *And at midnight Paul and Silas prayed, and sang praises unto God: and the prisoners heard them. And suddenly there was a great earthquake, so that the foundations of the prison were shaken: and immediately all the doors were opened, and every one's bands were loosed.* (Acts 16:25-26)

2) PRAISE FOR VENGENACE: Any vengeance prayers for GOD's timely intervention must be done righteously and judiciously. It is an understanding of your PRAISE that provokes God to react. You will never stand out until understanding comes into your life. I call that understanding LIGHT FROM HEAVEN. *The entrance of thy words giveth light; it giveth understanding unto the simple.* (Psalm 119:130) *Let the high praises of God be in their mouth, and a two-edged sword in their hand; To execute vengeance upon the heathen, and punishments upon the people.* (Psalm 149:6-7) Perhaps you have prayed about your oppressors and contenders. But until you begin to give God quality praise with righteous reasons, God is not permitted to come down with any vengeance verdict and punishment against your oppressors. Apostle Paul admonished us in Romans 12:19, *Dearly beloved, avenge not yourselves, but rather give place unto wrath: for it is written.* **Vengeance is mine; I will repay, saith the Lord.**

Chapter 1 — The Forces of Vengeance

O Lord God, to whom vengeance belongeth;
O God, to whom vengeance belongeth, shew thyself.
Psalm 94:1

3) PRAISE FOR VICTORY: Whenever we praise GOD for VICTORY, we praise GOD for VENGEANCE. *And it came to pass at the seventh time, when the priests blew with the trumpets, Joshua said unto the people, Shout; for the LORD hath given you the city.* (Joshua 6:16) *So the people shouted when the priests blew with the trumpets: and it came to pass, when the people heard the sound of the trumpet, and the people shouted with a great shout, that the wall fell down flat, so that the people went up into the city, every man straight before him, and they took the city.* (Joshua 6:20)

4) PRAISE FOR JUDGMENT: God is the judge of all the earth. Abraham said concerning God in Genesis 18:25: *That be far from thee to do after this manner, to slay the righteous with the wicked: and that the righteous should be as the wicked, that be far from thee:* **Shall not the Judge of all the earth do right?** The most high God executes judgment upon the heathen and punishment upon the wicked and unrighteous people. *To execute upon them the judgment written: this honour have all his saints. Praise ye the LORD.* (Psalms 149:9) *And when they began to sing and to praise, the LORD set ambushments against the children of Ammon, Moab, and mount Seir, which were come against Judah; and they were smitten.* (2 Chronicles 20:22)

And when Jehoshaphat and his people came to take

away the spoil of them, they found among them in abundance both riches with the dead bodies, and precious jewels, which they stripped off for themselves, more than they could carry away: and they were three days in gathering of the spoil, it was so much.
2 Chronicles 20:25

WHAT ARE THE WEAPONS OF VENGEANCE?

BOLD DECLARATION

Long time therefore abode they speaking boldly in the Lord, which gave testimony unto the word of his grace, and granted signs and wonders to be done by their hands.
ACTS 14:3

Speaking out BOLDLY in FAITH and in PRAYERS is a weapon of vengeance. As long as your mouth is closed, your case is closed. *For I will give you a mouth and wisdom, which all your adversaries shall not be able to gainsay nor resist.* (Luke 21:15)

WHO IS RESONSIBLE FOR ALL THE ASSAULTS?

> *But while men slept, his enemy came and sowed tares among the wheat, and went his way.*
> **Matthew 13:25**

The whole plot of the devil is to use SIN to eliminate us from having the access to provoke the wrath of GOD through vengeance. As long as we live in SIN, there is nothing THE SPIRIT OF GOD will do for us. Most SINNERS end up in misery, in shame and in defeat. Until we come out of SIN, we will never activate the ANGER OF GOD through vengeance prayers. The devil is responsible for all the troubles and attacks we have ever suffered in life.

> *He said unto them, an enemy hath done this.*
> **Matthew 13:28**

SIN will distract and disconnect us from provoking the wrath of the vengeance GOD. The enemy uses the pleasure of SIN to disconnect us from enjoying the privilege of activating the forces of vengeance.

Let's briefly examine sin.

WHAT IS SIN?

One man said S.I.N means Satan Identification Number, but it is incomplete in my own interpretation. In my own definition, sin is disobeying God Words and Commandments. Every time you operate outside of the commandment of God, you are committing sin. *He that committeth sin is of the devil; for the devil sinneth from the beginning. For this purpose the Son of God was manifested, that he might destroy the works of the devil.* (1 John 3:8)

> *He that covereth his sins shall not prosper:*
> *but whoso confesseth and forsaketh them*
> *shall have mercy.*
> **Proverbs 28:13**

Sin is the strongest force that stops the breakthrough and deliverance of anyone. A lot of us in the FAITH have misinterpreted and misguided this truth. No matter how we define it, evil is evil, what is wrong is wrong and what is good is good. *The evil bow before the good.* (Proverbs 14:19)

Despite what David said in Psalm 51:3—*For I acknowledge my transgressions: and my sin is ever before me*—man was born in sin like David attested. *Behold I was shapen in iniquity; and in sin did my mother conceive me.* (Psalm 51:5) It's sin that made our heart evil.

WHO IS A SINNER?

We are all born sinners, but whosoever confesses and forsakes their sins, GOD shall have mercy. There is a PREVAILING POWER that keeps us in SIN. ***For sin shall not have dominion over you: for ye are not under the law, but under grace.*** (Romans 6:14) Until such forces are crushed, it has power to prevail over the life of the believer. It's time to tell ourselves the truth. Is there any hidden sinful lifestyle we are dealing with? Confess it and crush it in the open with prayers. We will never stand a chance to activate the forces of vengeance with sin active in our lives.

Examine yourselves, whether ye be in the faith;
prove your own selves. Know ye not your own selves,
how that Jesus Christ is in you, except ye be reprobates?
2 Corinthians 13:5

Although most faith people live in denial about the work of the flesh, from my own scriptural understanding, everyone operating within the scope of Galatians 5:19-21 is classified as a sinner.

Now the works of the flesh are manifest, which are
these; Adultery, fornication, uncleanness, lasciviousness,
idolatry, witchcraft, hatred, variance, emulations, wrath,
strife, seditions, heresies, envyings, murders, drunken-
ness, revellings, and such like: of the which I tell you be-
fore, as I have also told you in time past, that they which
do such things shall not inherit the kingdom of God.
Galatians 5:19-21

Further supporting scripture…

But the fearful, and unbelieving,
and the abominable, and murderers,
and whoremongers, and sorcerers, and idolaters,

*and all liars, shall have their part in the lake
which burneth with fire and brimstone:
which is the second death.*
Revelation 21:8

WHO, THEREFORE, IS A SINNER?

1) Unbelievers: In my own view, all that have not acknowledged Jesus Christ as Lord and savior are sinners. The Bible says God heareth not sinners. Without contradiction, all unbelievers live in a sinful lifestyle. Unless God has mercy, most unbelievers will not make eternity in heaven.

2) Lies: All lies are sinners before the Almighty God. Lying is a very serious sin, simply because it leads to poverty and shame. Lying decays great destiny and erodes potential future. Someone whom I know very well lies so much to themselves they became a beggar by paralyzing their future, frustrating the will of God over their life.

HOW DO I COME OUT OF SIN?

Controlling SINFUL HABITS does not easily stop. Unless we are taking action by faith, those evil forces will continue to prevail and remote control our lives and destinies.

WE must **REPENT** and **CONFESS** and **PRO-**

CLAIM THE LORD JESUS CHRIST.

The word says, *"as many as received him, to them gave he power to become the sons of God, even to them that believe on his name."* (John 1:12)

To qualify for divine visitation, do the following sincerely:

1) Acknowledge that you are a sinner and that He died for you. (Romans 3:23)
2) Repent of your sins. (Acts 3:19, Luke 13:5, 2 Peter 3:9)
3) Believe in your heart that Jesus died for your sin. (Romans 10:10)
4) Confess Jesus as the Lord over your life. (Romans 10:10, Acts 2:21)

NOW REPEAT THIS PRAYER AFTER ME:

"Lord Jesus, I accept you today, as my Lord and my savior. Forgive me of my sins, wash me with your blood. Right now, I believe I am sanctified, I am saved, I am free. I am free from the power of sin to serve the Lord Jesus. Thank you Lord for saving me. Amen."

Congratulations.

YOU ARE NOW A BORN AGAIN CHRISTIAN!

STEPS TO OVERCOME THE LIFESTYLE OF SIN

1) REPENT: We must repent of all our sinful ways that do not please God. Whenever we repent, God will restore our lives. We must desire genuine salvation. We must live morally and ethically right in the sight of all men. Genuine salvation has no alternative with God.

2) FAITH: No one will overcome any sinful lifestyle without faith. FAITH IN GOD is the force that will help anyone come out of sin. Most SINFUL HABITS will not suddenly stop—UNLESS THE SPIRIT OF FAITH OVERCOMES OUR SINFUL DESIRES. Unless we develop faith in GOD, sinful forces have the power to prevail. Therefore, develop faith that will crush all prevailing sinful habits in Jesus name. I see your faith bringing you deliverance over that prevailing SINFUL LIFESTYLE.

3) DECISIONS: *...therefore choose life, that both thou and thy seed may live.* (Deuteronomy 30:19) Whenever we truly decide to come out of sin, sin has no power to prevail against our lives. Decisions are the STRONGHOLD to COME OUT OF SIN. Most of the things that happened in our lifetime are directly related to the decision we made. Decisions are the gateway into our freedom, liberty and a glorious future. Despite all the riches of the father, the prodigal son took a drastic decision that reduced him to eat the pig's food, until he came to himself. (Luke 15:17) Although you might not have noticed nor considered these; your lifestyle REVOLVES AROUND the decisions you make daily. Whatever present challenge you are dealing with, it did not happen overnight. At some point in your lifetime, you made a decision and invited certain SINFUL forces into your life. Make a decision today and evict the old man of sin. (See Romans 6:1-14)

4) PRAYER: Prayer is necessary, especially when dealing with the lifestyle of SIN. It takes a man of PRAYER to overcome SINFUL HABITS. Ninety-nine percent of our changed lifestyle becomes our permanent character over time because of our PRAYER LIFESTYLE. The place of prayer cannot be overemphasized in our lives. PRAYER CHANGES THE WAY WE SEE THINGS, PRAYER CHANGES HOW WE REACT TO THINGS WITHIN AND AROUND US.

HOW TO DEVELOP A PRAYER LIFESTYLE

We must believe in God. We must start our daily routine with prayers.

1) Join a prayer fellowship.

2) Develop your personal prayer life.

3) Read prayer literatures.

4) Make friends with men and women of prayer.

5) Believe in the ministration and help of the Holy Spirit.

6) Allow God to have dominion over the affairs of your life.

7) Trust in God at all times.

8) Expect God to manifest every time you pray.

SUMMARY OF CHAPTER ONE

Alexander the coppersmith did me much evil: the Lord reward him according to his works.
2 Timothy 4:14

—We must all understand how to provoke God's vengeance on any person. We must know that vengeance is a righteous thing with God.

—It is our kingdom obligation to provoke the wrath of God on the platform of righteousness.

—Although we would love revenge on our oppositions, vengeance simply belongs to God.

—Without the justification of righteousness, our vengeance God will do nothing.

—Sin is a hindrance that will stop the recompense of tribulation from God, to them that trouble us.

—We must enforce the laws of the spirit by the blood of Jesus.

—We must pray violently to activate the finger of God in any prevailing matter.

CHAPTER 2
OVERCOMING
THE TRIBULATIONS OF LIFE

These things I have spoken unto you, that in me ye might have peace. In the world ye shall have tribulation: but be of good cheer; I have overcome the world.
John 16:33

We must all come to the reality that we must keep fighting for everything in this race of life. We live in an evil time when men will kill each other for money and for real estate land disputes. To overcome the tribulation of life we must develop inner strength, patience, and endurance to deal with the adversary the devil. Recall Apostle Paul story.

Thrice was I beaten with rods, once was I stoned, thrice I suffered shipwreck, a night and a day I have been in the deep; In journeyings often, in perils of waters, in perils of robbers, in perils by mine own countrymen, in perils by the heathen, in perils in the city, in perils in the wilderness, in perils in the sea, in perils among false brethren; In weariness and painfulness, in watchings often, in hunger and thirst, in fastings often, in cold and nakedness.
2 Corinthians 11:25-27

Chapter 2   Overcoming the Tribulations of Life

Although tribulations of life is also inherited, in most cases we determine our fate in our lifetime. It is our FAITH in GOD that determines our FATE in LIFE.

Some of us were born into very poor families. As a result, we settled for poverty in our lifetime. Others were born into very rich families, but became extremely poor in their lifetime. "Life is not fair." You only get what you are ready to fight for in life.

WHAT ARE THE TRIBULATIONS OF LIFE?

The tribulations of life are stronghold designed STOP us from making eternity with CHRIST JESUS IN HEAVEN. All those PREVAILING OBSTACLES OF LIFE ARE DESIGNED TO TEST OUR FAITH IN GOD.

He that hath an ear, let him hear what the Spirit saith unto the churches; He that overcometh shall not be hurt of the second death.
Revelation 2:11

Most of us have allowed prevailing obstacles and the challenges of life to remote and manipulate our destinies.

He that hath an ear, let him hear what the Spirit saith unto the churches; To him that overcometh will I give

to eat of the hidden manna, and will give him a white stone, and in the stone a new name written, which no man knoweth saving he that receiveth it.
Revelation 2:17

WHAT ARE THE CHALLENEGES OF LIFE?

A challenge is an obstacle, or a prevailing problem that hinders a person from attaining his or her goal in life. Jesus said, **"But be of good cheer; I have overcome the world."**

There are plenty of challenges that confront us today in our everyday life. Many people dropped out of college because they either lack sufficient funds to pay for tuition. OR because they were not smart enough to pass the classroom exams. Many women married, but could not give birth to a child. Others just cannot find someone who will marry them.

Regardless of how we examine the above examples of circumstances, they are all examples of the challenges of life.

We are commanded by scriptures to rejoice in our tribulation, because trials are permitted by God to build strength and endurance inside of us. We must all develop self-confidence and patience in GOD in order to overcome any prevailing obstacle in life. Life Challenges come to different people in different ways. TO OVERCOME THE TRIBULATIONS OF LIFE, WE MUST TOTALLY DEPEND, TRUST AND HAVE

FAITH IN GOD.

WE MUST DEVELOP WINNER'S MENTALITY IN OUR MIND

Those who quit easily in the race of life never achieve anything. One man said, "You cannot climb the ladder of success dressed in the costume of failure." I admonish you to develop a mentality of never quitting, regardless of the circumstances surrounding you.

"WINNERS NEVER QUIT"

For a just man falleth seven times, and riseth up again...
Proverbs 24:16

Fanny J. Crosby was a renowned hymn writer who became blind when she was only six weeks old. But against all odds and through her faith in Christ, she became one of the greatest hymn writers the world has ever known. THE WORST THING THAT WILL HAPPEN TO ANYONE IS TO GIVE UP AND QUIT IN THE RACE OF LIFE.

THOSE WHO QUIT NEVER WIN IN THE RACE OF LIFE

Abraham Lincoln prevailed against all odds

and became the 16th President of The United States of America. Bible characters like Paul, David, Joseph, Daniel, Abraham and many others prevailed against all obstacles in their lives. The champion inside all of us will never emerge unless we overcome trials and tribulations in life. Nobody knew DAVID until he defeated and killed GOLIATH, the champion of the Philistines.

"If there is no trial, there will be no triumphs." "If there is no triumphs, there is no trophy." ***"Know ye not that they which run in a race run all, but one receiveth the prize? So run, that ye may obtain."*** (1 Corinthians 9:24)

GOLD does not emerge unless it is processed through the furnace. Job said, *"But he knoweth the way that I take: when he hath tried me, I shall come forth as gold."* (Job 23:10)

WHAT TO DO IN TIME OF PREVAILING OBSTACLES?

HAVE FAITH IN GOD

It is our faith in God that will uphold us, especially in times of trials. We must all develop confidence in ourselves and FAITH in GOD. (SEE MARK 11:20.)

CONFIDENCE IN OURSELVES

We must develop a lifestyle of self-confidence in any discipline we find pleasure in doing. Without self-confidence we will never be able to accomplish any task in life.

BELIEVE IN GOD

Jesus said, "Do not be afraid, only believe." The Bible admonished us to look unto Jesus, who is the Author and the Finisher of our faith. (See Hebrews 12:2.) The ultimate example of overcoming tribulation is the death of Jesus Christ on the Cross. Jesus therefore gave us an example of how to endure life's trials by travelling with the cross to Calvary and by dying on the Cross. As long as we believe GOD, there is no tribulation that will succumb us in this race of life.

WE MUST FOCUS ON GOD

Although Joseph persevered through numerous obstacles in his life, he was focused on the reality of the dream GOD gave him as a youth. Along the journey of his life, JOSEPH went into prison. But through the help of God and by remaining focused and positive in his life, he was able to overcome. Talking about JOSEPH, the Bible said, *"Until the time that his word came: the word of the Lord tried him."* (Psalm 105:19) *And God sent me before you to preserve you a posterity in the earth, and to save your lives by a great deliverance.* (Genesis 45:7)

THE HELP OF THE HOLY SPIRIT

There is no substitute for the help of the HOLY SPIRIT, especially in times of trial and tribulation. It is reasonable to request the help of God and the help of others in times of trial and tribulation. The Bible says in Psalm 46:1 that *"God is our refuge and strength, a very present help in trouble."* David, Joseph and Paul are typical examples of men in the Bible who encountered numerous challenges in their lifetime, but they were quick to always cry out to God for help.

Our most referenced example is Joseph, who solicited the help of the butler while in the jail. Do not refrain from telling people about your obstacles and shortcomings in life. You will be amazed whom GOD will use to deliver you from such problems. Clement W. Stone once said, "Tell everybody what you want to do and someone will help you do it."

ENDURANCE

The Bible says in Mark 13:13, *"And ye shall be hated of all men for my name's sake: but he that shall endure unto the end, the same shall be saved."* Endurance is the platform for overwhelming victory against all the tribulations of life. Psalm 30:5 tells us that "weeping may endure for a night, but joy comes in the morning." Jesus endured the pain of the Cross. Joseph, Paul and Silas endured the torture of imprisonment. We are also called to endure the pain that comes with trial. (See Mark 13:13.)

Our victory over any prevailing challenge is not assured—unless we are ready to endure the torture and the pains, regardless of the deplorable circumstances.

ENCOURAGE YOURSELF

Chapter 2 Overcoming the Tribulations of Life

And David was greatly distressed; for the people spake of stoning him, because the soul of all the people was grieved, every man for his sons and for his daughters: ***but David encouraged himself in the Lord his GOD.***
1 Samuel 30:6

The HOLY SPIRIT desires that we encourage ourselves in times of trial. Oftentimes we underestimate what GOD can do, through others, for us—and through us, for ourselves and for others.

WE MUST BE AT PEACE WITH OURSELVES AND WITH OTHERS

The PEACE of GOD is a VIRTUE that has no secondhand value. We are encouraged by scriptures to be at PEACE with all MEN. God says we should *"follow peace with all men, and holiness, without which no man will see the Lord."* (Hebrews 12:14) We must first be at peace with ourselves before we can be at peace with others. It is the PEACE of GOD that will CALM the STORMS OF LIFE. (Tribulation.) The PEACE of GOD grants us the assurance of the HOLY SPIRIT, who is our very present help in times of trouble.

DEPEND ON GOD'S GRACE

In my own understanding, "GOD's GRACE equals GOD's FAVOR." It is this GRACE (GOD'S FAVOR) that will overcome all trials. The GRACE of

GOD upon our lives must be present in times of trials. It is GOD's GRACE in times of trouble that will overcome the prevailing tribulation in our lives. Apostle Paul refused to accept his trials and prayed to GOD to remove his trouble. But God said to him, *"my grace is sufficient for thee."* (2 Corinthians 12:9) His strength is perfected in our weakness. We must overcome trials and tribulations in life before we can qualify to counsel anyone. I see you overcoming your present challenge in life in the name of Jesus Christ.

WE MUST BE BORN AGAIN

You cannot engage GOD's help unless you are genuinely born again. Whenever you are born again, you become a child of GOD. The Bible says commit your ways to GOD, TRUST also in HIM. GOD will rescue your life from whatever evil prevailing forces are hindering your breakthroughs in life. *Jesus answered and said unto him, verily, verily, I say unto thee, except a man be born again, he cannot see the kingdom of God. Nicodemus saith unto him, how can a man be born when he is old? Can he enter the second time into his mother's womb, and be born? Jesus answered, Verily, verily, I say unto thee, except a man be born of water and of the Spirit, he cannot enter into the kingdom of God. That which is born of the flesh is flesh; and that which is born of the Spirit is spirit. Marvel not that I said unto thee, Ye must be born again. The wind bloweth where it listeth, and thou hearest the sound thereof, but canst not tell whence it cometh, and whither it goeth: so is every one that is born of the Spirit.* (John 3:3-8)

REVIEW OF CHAPTER TWO

—We must encourage ourselves in the Lord if we are to prevail in life.

—We must tackle every obstacle in life with faith in God, believing that we must prevail at the end of the problem.

—You are bigger than any obstacle the devil will fabricate in your life.

—We must develop a possibility mentality against all obstruction and hindering forces of life.

—We must comprehend that every champion MUST put up a fight before he or she emerges.

—Irrespective of what you are going through in life, tell people that matter in your life about it.

—As believers, quitting is never an option for us.

—We must endure trial to triumph in the race of life.

DECISION KEYS

1) Nothing changes until you make up your mind.

2) Decision is the gateway to deliverance.

3) Until you decide, no one will decide for you.

4) Your prosperity is proportional to your decisions.

5) The decision you make will determine the future you'll create.

6) Decision creates future and fulfills destinies.

7) Decision beautifies our future.

8) Decision keeps you out of trouble.

9) Decision exempts you from evil.

10) Decision guarantees eternity.

11) You can only go far in life by your faith decisions.

12) You are poor because you made poor decisions.

13) Make a decision and change your life.

14) Life-changing decisions are a function of quality

information.

15) Success in life is a function of decision.

16) Life experience is full of decisions.

17) Decisions change destinies.

18) Never settle for information—only look for revelation.

19) You are where you are today based on your last decision.

20) Information is crucial in decision-making.

21) Decision makers rule the world.

22) You can rule your world by quality decisions.

23) As long as you decide rightly, Satan cannot harass you.

CHAPTER 3
CONQUERING THE FORCES OF WICKEDNESS

Be not overcome of evil, but overcome evil with good.
ROMANS 12:21

We live in an evil generation, where men take glory for doing wickedness. A lot of men and women are into ritual killings, the occcult and all sorts of secret societies. On a very slow but steady pace, doing wickedness is becoming the norm of the day. We are gradually engrafting wickedness as an everyday thing. *The evil bow before the good; and the wicked at the gates of the righteous.* (Proverbs 14:19)

And we know that we are of God,
and the whole world lieth in wickedness.
1 JOHN 5:19

The forces of wickedness must be confronted and conquered. Oh let the wickedness of the wicked come to an end; but establish the just: for the righteous God trieth the hearts and reins. (Psalm 7:9) So many evil men and women have taken advantage to continue doing evil as long as they live and exist. *Because sentence against an evil work is not executed speedily, therefore the heart of the sons of men is fully set in them to do evil.* (Ecclesiastes 8:11)

> *But it shall not be well with the wicked,*
> *neither shall he prolong his days, which are as a shadow;*
> *because he feareth not before God.*
> **Ecclesiastes 8:13**

Wickedness, no matter how we define it, is not right in the sight of God and in the sight of men. It MUST come to and end.

HOW DO I CONQUER THE FORCES OF WICKEDNESS?

> *Nay, in all these things we are more than conquerors*
> *through him that loved us.*
> **Romans 8:37**

Among the strong forces that secured our victory against the wickedness of the wicked are the forces of faith, new birth, righteousness, boldness and **FAITH**.

FAITH IS OUR DEFENCE.

> *Above all, taking the shield of faith, wherewith ye shall be*
> *able to quench all the fiery darts of the wicked*
> **EPHESIANS 6:16**

With the shield of FAITH, we are protected

against the devil's wiles and schemes. As long as we speak faith into our circumstances, the devil has no chance to prevail against our lives. It takes the mystery of faith to understand the revelation of "greater is he that is in you, than he that is in the world."

FAITH IS OUR VICTORY CERTIFICATION.

For whatsoever is born of God overcometh the world: and this is the victory that overcometh the world, even our faith.
1 JOHN 5:4

We do not stand a chance to conquer the wickedness of the wicked, unless we position ourselves by FAITH. Faith is our anchor to conquer all the brutal attacks of the wicked. OUR FAITH IN GOD is the mystery that will subdue and overcome the wicked one—the devil.

NEW BIRTH—WE MUST BE BORN AGAIN

If we must conquer the forces of wickedness, we must be born again!

As long as you are not born again, you will be walking in ignorance and in sin. We must all set the record straight by receiving genuine salvation. We must confess and believe the lord Jesus Christ.

BOLDNESS

Never allow the devil's wiles and schemes to

intimidate you with fear. "What you do not confront, you cannot conquer." We must conquer the forces of wickedness by confronting it with boldness in spirit and in truth.

RIGHTEOUS LIFESTYLE

...but he that maketh haste to be rich shall not be innocent.
Proverbs 28:20

We cannot CONQUER THE FORCES OF WICKEDNESS by doing evil. RIGHTEOUSNESS as a lifestyle means doing what is RIGHT in the sight of GOD and in the sight of MEN. *The evil bow before the good; and the wicked at the gates of the righteous.* (Proverbs 14:19)

AGREEMENT

Can two walk together, except they be agreed?
Amos 3:3

We must walk in agreement with the HOLY SPIRIT to CONQUER THE FORCES OF WICKEDNESS. *Verily I say unto you, Whatsoever ye shall bind on earth shall be bound in heaven: and whatsoever ye shall loose on earth shall be loosed in heaven. Again I say unto you, That if two of you shall agree on earth as touching anything that they shall ask, it shall be done for them of my Father which is in heaven. For where two or three are gathered together in my name, there am I in the midst of them.* (Matthew 18:18-20)

THE RIGHT WORDS

How forcible are right words!...
Job 6:25

We must speak the Right words to CONQUER THE FORCES OF WICKEDNESS.

SOUL WINNING

And Jesus came and spake unto them, saying,
All power is given unto me in heaven and in earth.
Go ye therefore, and teach all nations, baptizing them
in the name of the Father, and of the Son, and of
the Holy Ghost: Teaching them to observe
all things whatsoever I have commanded you:
and, lo, I am with you always,
even unto the end of the world. Amen.
Matthew 2 8:18-20

Most evil men do evil because they have never heard the gospel of Jesus Christ. Some people commit wickedness because it is their tradition. We must CONQUER THE FORCES OF WICKEDNESS by spreading the gospel of Jesus Christ and by WINNING SOULS for the KINGDOM OF GOD.

OBEDIENCE

We must obey the PRESENCE and LEADING of the HOLY SPIRIT to CONQUER THE FORCES OF WICKEDNESS. It is the POWER of the HOLY SPIRIT that will CONQUER all FORCES OF WICKEDNESS. Remember the HOLY SPIRIT is the seal of Redemption. In whom ye also trusted, after that ye heard the word of truth, the gospel of your salvation: in whom also after that ye believed, ye were sealed with that holy Spirit of promise. (Ephesians 1:13) Obey them that have the rule over you, and submit yourselves: for they watch for your souls, as they that must give account, that they may do it with joy, and not with grief: for that is unprofitable for you. (Hebrews 13:17)

PRAY IN THE SPIRIT

PRAYER is the strongest weapon to CONQUER THE FORCES OF WICKEDNESS. There is no substitute for PRAYING in the SPIRIT. When we pray in the SPIRIT, we are not speaking to MEN but unto GOD. And WHEN GOD TAKES OVER, THAT BATTLE BECOMES OVER. *For he that speaketh in an unknown tongue speaketh not unto men, but unto God: for no man understandeth him; howbeit in the spirit he speaketh mysteries.* (1 Corinthians 14:2)

CHAPTER 4
PRAYER OF SALVATION

Have you accepted Jesus Christ as your personal Lord and Savior?

WHAT IS SALVATION?

Salvation means deliverance from our sins and sickness and redemption of our soul. There is no other way we all can be saved except by the name of Jesus Christ of Nazareth.

Neither is there salvation in any other: for there is none other name under heaven given among men, whereby we must be saved.
ACTS 4:12

I am glad you have read this book all the way from the beginning to this point. All I have said from the beginning will remain a mystery until you commit it into practice.

What must I do to receive SALVATION?

To RECEIVE salvation, you must be BORN AGAIN.

The word says as many as received Him, to them gave He power to become the sons of God. Even to them that believe on His name. To qualify as a

BORN AGAIN CHRISTIAN you must sincerely—

> 1) Acknowledge that you are a sinner and that He died for you. (Romans 3:23)
> 2) Repent of your sins. (Acts 3:19, Luke 13:5, 2 Peter 3:9)
> 3) Believe in your heart that Jesus died for your sins. (Romans 10:10)
> 4) Confess Jesus as the Lord over your life. (Romans 10:10, Acts 2:21)

Now repeat this prayer after me:

Say Lord Jesus, I accept you today, as my Lord and my savior. Forgive me of my sins, wash me with your blood. Right now, I believe I am sanctified, I am saved, I am free. I am free from the power of sin, to serve the Lord Jesus. Thank you Lord for saving me. Amen.

Congratulations. You are now...

A BORN AGAIN CHRISTIAN.

Again I say to you—CONGRATULATIONS!

I adjure you to watch the Spirit of God bear witness with your Spirit, confirming His word with signs following. The word says The Spirit itself beareth witness with our spirit, that we are the children of God.

CONCLUSION

Dearly beloved, avenge not yourselves, but rather give place unto wrath: for it is written, Vengeance is mine; I will repay, saith the Lord.
Romans 12:19

Although vengeance belongs to God, we must activate the anger of God appropriately. Without righteousness, boldness and spiritual violence, God's anger for the infliction of punishment in return for a wrong retribution will not be effective.

God is jealous, and the Lord revengeth; the Lord revengeth, and is furious; the Lord will take vengeance on his adversaries, and he reserveth wrath for his enemies.
Nahum 1:2

Let us hear the conclusion of the whole matter: Fear God, and keep his commandments: for this is the whole duty of man. For God shall bring every work into judgment, with every secret thing, whether it be good, or whether it be evil.
Ecclesiastes 12:13-14

The ANGER of God is provoked only when we keep HIS commandments. The Bible says in Ecclesiastes: 12:14, *"For God shall bring every work into judgment, with every secret thing, whether it be good, or whether it be evil."* If you are not a born again Christian, we can help you here receive genuine salvation.

Therefore if any man be in Christ, he is a new creature: old things are passed away; behold, all things are become new.
2 Corinthians 5:17

I adjure you to watch the Spirit of God bear witness with your Spirit confirming His word with signs following. The word says The Spirit itself beareth witness with our spirit, that we are the children of God. Join a Bible-believing church or join us on our Wednesdays healing and Sunday miracle worship services at 343 Sanford Avenue, Newark, New Jersey 07106.

WISDOM KEYS

—If you train your mind to reason, it will train your hands to earn money.

—It is absurd to use the money of the heathen to build the kingdom of the living God.

—Every Ministry reveals its agenda and VISION either at the beginning or at the end.

—Be careful of your life. It is your First Ministry.

—Everyone is waiting for you to change your mind. Until you change your thinking, nothing changes around you.

—Multiple academic degrees in other disciplines gave me the chance to think and reason.

—Whatever anyone is thinking at any time reveals what is inside of their heart.

—All planned events are the product of meditation.

—Every event is designed for a designated timeline.

—Wisdom is your ability to think, to create and invent.

— If you can think wisely enough, you will come out of debt.

—The distance between you and your success is your innovative and creative ability to think well.

—Success is the result of hard work, commitment, resolve and determined learning from past mistakes and failings.

—If you organize your mind, you have organized your life and destiny.

—There is a thin line between success and failure.

Chapter 4   Prayer of Salvation

—Wealth is your ability to think, power is your ability to reason and success is your ability to be informed.

—If you can make use of your mind by thinking and reasoning, God will make use of your life and destiny.

—Reflect, reason, think and be Great.

—Famous people are born of woman.

—That you will make it is your intention, that you will survive is your resolve, that you will succeed with changes is your determination, personal efforts and hard work.

—No man was born a failure.

—Lack of vision is the result of failure.

—Working with mental patients encourages and aspire me to be a productive observant and dedicated to my assignment.

—Successful people are not magicians. It is the will-power, combined with hard work and determination and a resolve to succeed, that make them succeed.

—In the unequivocal state of the mind, intention is not a location or a position. It is the state of the mind.

—So many people think that they think.

—The mind is used to think, to reflect and to reason.

—You will remain blind with your eyes open until you can see with your mind by thinking.

—There is no favoritism in accurate and precise calculation.

—Although knowledge is power, information is the key and gateway to a great future.

—It will take the hand of God to move the hand of man.

—With the backing of the great wise God, nothing will disconnect you from your inheritance.

—As long as you have wisdom and understanding of God, Satan and evil cannot manipulate your life and destiny.

—You have come this far in life by your own judgment and the decisions you made in the past. Now lean in and listen to God for another dimension of greatness.

—Great people are ordinary people. It is extra ordinary efforts and the price of sacrifice that produces greatness in them.

—As a mental direct care worker, I saw a great pastor and a motivational speaker within myself.

—A menial job does not reduce your self-worth. Until you resolve to achieve greatness and see greatness in all you do, you will never count in your community.

—The principle of Jesus will solve your gambling and addiction problems.

—The man of Jesus will lead you into heaven.

—Everyone has their self-appraisal and what they think about you. Until you discover yourself, other opinions about you will alter the real you.

—Supervisors and directors are just positions in the chain of command in a work place.

—Never allow your supervisor on a job to alter your opinion about yourself.

—Everyone can come out of debt if they make up their mind.

—The fact that I am not a decision-maker at my work place does not diminish my contribution to my world.

—Self-encouragement and determination is a resolve of the heart.

—If you are determined to make a difference and do the things that make a difference, you will eventually make a difference.

—Good things do not come easy.

—Short cuts will cut your life short.

—Those who look ahead move ahead.

—Life is all about making an impact. In your lifetime strive to make an impact in your community.

—Make friends and connect with people who are moving ahead of you in life.

—If you can look around well, you have come a long way in your life, made a lot of difference and realized a lot of success in life.

—If you are my old friend, hurry up to reach out to me before I become a stranger to you.

—I am blessed with inspirations from God that changed my interpretation of the world around me.

—I thought I was stagnant and lonely until I looked around and noticed my children running around and my wife cooking in the kitchen.

—You will be a better person if you understand the characteristics of your personality like your mood swings, attitudes and habits.

—It is the seed of love you sow into the heart of a child and a woman that you reap in due time.

—Love is not selfish.

—Love shares everything, including the concealed secrets of the mind.

—As long as you have a prayer life and a Bible, you will never feel lonely in the race of life.

—When good friends disconnect from you, let them go. They might have seen something new in a different direction.

—Confidence in yourself and in God is the only way to bring you out of captivity

—Never train a child to waste his or her time.

—The mind is the greatest asset of a great future.

—You walk by common sense, run by principles and fly by instruction.

—Those who become successful in life did it by self-determination, hard work and learning from past failures.

—Most successful people are lonely people. No one renders help to them, believing they are already successful. Except when they seek for more knowledge and information, they are all alone.

—I exercise my judgment and make a decision every minute of the day. Decisions are crucial, critical and vital with reference to your future.

—So many people wish for a great future. You can only work towards a great future.

—Your celebrity status began when you discovered your talent. What are you good at? Work at it with all your commitment.

—Prayers will sustain you, but the wisdom of God will prosper you.

—When I met Oyedepo, his teachings changed my perspective. But when I met Ibiyeomie, his teaching changed my perception.

MIRACLE CARE OUTREACH

*"...But that the members should have
the same care one for another"*
1 Corinthians 12:25

We are all members of the body of Christ. Jesus commanded us to love our neighbor as ourselves. This includes caring for one another as a member of one body. True love is expressed in caring and giving. The word says, for God so Love He gave....

Reach out to someone in need of Jesus. Help someone in crisis find Christ. Look out and prove your love to Jesus by caring and inviting your friends and associates to find Jesus the Healer.

Invite your friends to our Home Care Cell Fellowship (Miracle Chapel Intl. Satellite Fellowship). We're in the U.S. at 33 Schley Street, Newark, New Jersey 07112. Home Care Cell Fellowship Group meets every Tuesday at 6:00pm-7:00pm.

If you are in Nigeria—MIRACLE OF GOD MINISTRIES, aka "MIRACLE CHAPEL INTL." Mpama–Egbu-Owerri Imo state Nigeria.

LIFE IS NOT ALL ABOUT DURATION, BUT IT'S ALL ABOUT DONATION

What does this statement mean?
Life consists not in accumulation of material

wealth. (Luke 12:15) But it's all about liberality...i.e., what you can give and share with others. (Proverbs 11:25) When you live for others, you live forever—because you outlive your generation by the legacy you leave behind after you depart into glory to be with the Lord. But when you live for yourself, when you are reduced to SELF—you are easily forgotten when you die and depart in glory.

Permit me to admonish you today to live your life to be a blessing to a soul connected to you today. I want you to know that so many souls are connected and looking up to you, and through you so many souls will be saved and rescued from destruction. Will you disciple someone today to find Jesus Christ?

As a genuine Christian, it is your duty to evangelize Jesus Christ to all you meet on your way. Jesus is still in the healing business—Jesus is still doing miracles, from time of old to now. Therefore, tell someone about Jesus Christ today, disciple and bring them to Church. *Philip findeth Nathanael...* (John 1:45)

Please prove the sincerity of your love for God today, please become a soul winner. The dignity of your Christianity is hidden in your boldness to proclaim and evangelize Jesus Christ to all you meet on your way. There is a question mark on the integrity of your Christianity until you become a life soul winner. Invite someone to join us worship the Lord Jesus this coming Sunday.

Chapter 4   Prayer of Salvation

MIRACLE OF GOD MINISTRIES
PILLARS OF THE COMMISSION

We Believe, Preach and Practice the following:

1) We believe and preach Salvation to every living human being.

2) We believe and preach Repentance and Forgiveness of sins.

3) We believe and preach the baptism of the Holy Spirit and Spiritual gifts.

4) We believe and teach Prosperity.

5) We believe and preach Divine Healing and Miracles—Signs and Wonder.

6) We believe and preach Faith.

7) We believe and proclaim the Power of God (Supernatural).

8) We believe and proclaim Praise and Worship to God.

9) We believe and preach Wisdom.

10) We believe and preach Holiness (Consecration).

11) We believe and preach Vision.

12) We believe and teach the Word of God.

13) We believe and teach Success.

14) We believe and practice Prayer.

15) We believe and teach Deliverance.

These 15 stones form the Pillars of Our Commission. Become part of this church family and follow this great move of God.

MY HEARTFELT PRAYER FOR YOU

It is my burning desire for God to touch you through one of our teaching books or CDs. It also my personal desire for you encounter God for yourself.

Now let me Pray for you:

O Lord God! I beseech thee, and through personal prayer intercession today that the Holy Spirit will touch the precious soul reading this book and turn their life around. Spirit of God, possess this loved one. Lord, overcome all dominating, controlling forces that have prevailed over their lives. I come against all oppressive thought, in Jesus Name. Henceforth, I pronounce you free from manipulation, intimidation and domination of the wicked enemy called the devil. You are free from all satanic harassment and assaults. Amen.

PROVOKE VENGEANCE AGAINST YOUR ENEMIES

Have you ever wondered why are you being oppressed, maltreated or molested by others?

Alexander the coppersmith did me much evil: the Lord reward him according to his works.
2 Timothy 4:14

Is there any mystery code of your life and blood pattern that you do not know?

Have you accepted the Lord Jesus as your lord and personal savior?

No matter how quick you want him to show up, you must repent. Because eternity is real, heaven is sure.

Therefore, turn unto God in supplication, in thanksgiving and in prayer, and God will turn in your favor.

ABOUT THE AUTHOR

Rev. Franklin N. Abazie is the founding and Presiding Pastor of Miracle of God Ministries, with headquarters in Newark, New Jersey USA and a branch church in Owerri-Imo State Nigeria. He is following the footsteps of one of his mentors, the healing evangelist Oral Roberts of the blessed memory. The Lord passed Oral Roberts' healing mantle two days before he went to be with the Lord at age 91 into the hands of healing evangelist Rev. Franklin N. Abazie in a vision.

In all his services, the Power and Presence of God is present to heal all in his audience. Rev. Abazie is an ordained man of God, with a Healing Ministry reviving the healing and miracle ministry of Jesus Christ of Nazareth.

Pastor Franklin N. Abazie, has been called by God with a unique mandate: **"THE MOMENT IS DUE TO IMPACT YOUR WORLD THROUGH THE REVIVAL OF THE HEALING AND MIRACLE MINISTRY OF JESUS CHRIST OF NAZARETH.**

"I AM SENDING YOU TO RESTORE HEALTH UNTO THEE AND I WILL HEAL THEE OF THY WOUNDS, SAID THE LORD OF HOST"

Rev. Abazie is a gifted, ardent teacher of the word of God, who operates also in the office of a Prophet, generating and attracting undeniable signs and wonders, special miracles and healings, with apostolic fireworks of the Holy Ghost. He is the founding and presiding senior Pastor of this fast growing Healing Ministry. He has written over 86 inspirational, healing and transforming books covering almost all aspects of divine healing and life. He is happily married and blessed with children.

BOOKS BY REV. FRANKLIN N. ABAZIE:

1) The Outcome of Faith
2) Understanding the Secret of Prevailing Prayers
3) Commanding Abundance

4) Understanding the Secret of the Man God Uses
5) Activating My Due Season
6) Overcoming Divine Verdicts
7) The Outcome of Divine Wisdom
8) Understanding God's Restoration Mandate
9) Walking In the Victory and Authority of the Truth
10) God's Covenant Exemption
11) Destiny Restoration Pillars
12) Provoking Acceptable Praise
13) Understanding Divine Judgment
14) Activating Angelic Re-enforcement
15) Provoking Un-Merited Favo
16) The Benefits of the Speaking Faith
17) Understanding Divine Arrangement
18) How to Keep Your Healing
19) Understanding the Mysteries of the Speaking Faith
20) Understanding the Mysteries of Prophetic Healing
21) Operating Under the Rules of Creative Healing
22) Understanding the Joy of Breakthrough
23) Understanding the Mystery of Breakthrough
24) Understanding Divine Prosperity
25) Understanding Divine Healing
26) Retaining Your Inheritance
27) Overcoming Confusing Spirit
28) Commanding Angelic Escorts
29) Enforcing Your Inheritance In Christ Jesus
30) Understanding Your Guardian Angels
31) Overcoming the Dominion of Sin
32) Understanding the Voice of God
33) The Outstanding Benefits of the Anointing

34) The Audacity of the Blood of Jesus
35) Walking in the Reality of the Anointing
36) Escaping the Nightmare of Poverty
37) Understanding Your Harvest Season
38) Activating Your Success Buttons
39) Overcoming the Forces of Darkness
40) Overcoming the Devices of the Devil
41) Overcoming Demonic Agents
42) Overcoming the Sorrows of Failure
43) Rejecting the Sorrows of Failure
44) Resisting the Sorrows of Poverty
45) Restoring Broken Marriages
46) Redeeming Your Days
47) The Force of Vision
48) Overcoming the Forces of Ignorance
49) Understanding the Sacrifice of Small Beginning
50) The Might of Small Beginning
51) Understanding the Mysteries of Prophesy
52) Overcoming Dream Nightmares
53) Breaking the Shackles of the Curse of the Law
54) Understanding the Joy of Harvest
55) Wisdom for Signs & Wonders
56) Wisdom for Generational Impact
57) Wisdom for Marriage Stability
58) Understanding the Number of Your Days
59) Enforcing Your Kingdom Rights
60) Escaping the Traps of Immoralities
61) Escaping the Trap of Poverty
62) Accessing Biblical Prosperity
63) Accessing True Riches in Christ

64) Silencing the Voice of the Accuser
65) Overcoming the Forces of Oppositions
66) Quenching the Voice of the Avenger
67) Silencing Demonic Prediction & Projection
68) Silencing Your Mocker
69) Understanding the Power of the Holy Ghost
70) Understanding the Baptism of Power
71) The Mystery of the Blood of Jesus
72) Understanding the Mystery of Sanctification
73) Understanding the Power of Holiness
74) Understanding the Forces of Purity & Righteousness
75) Activating the Forces of Vengeance
76) Appreciating the Mystery of Restoration
77) Overcoming the Projection & Prediction of the Enemy
78) Engaging the Mystery of the Blood
79) Commanding the Power of the Speaking Faith
80) Uprooting the Forces Against Your Rising
81) Overcoming Mere Success Syndrome
82) Understanding Divine Sentence
83) Understanding the Mystery of Praise
84) Understanding the Author of Faith
85) The Mystery of the Finisher of Faith
86) Attracting Supernatural Favor

MIRACLE OF GOD MINISTRIES

NIGERIA CRUSADE   2012

MIRACLE OF GOD MINISTRIES
NIGERIA CRUSADE
2012

MIRACLE OF GOD MINISTRIES
NIGERIA CRUSADE 2012

MIRACLE OF GOD MINISTRIES

NIGERIA CRUSADE

2012

MIRACLE OF GOD MINISTRIES

NIGERIA CRUSADE

2012

www.ingramcontent.com/pod-product-compliance
Lightning Source LLC
Chambersburg PA
CBHW021449080526
44588CB00009B/756